Great Americans

Frederick Douglass

Barbara Kiely Miller

Reading consultant: Susan Nations, M.Ed., author/literacy coach/ consultant in literacy development

WEEKLY READER®
PUBLISHING

Please visit our web site at: www.garethstevens.com
For a free color catalog describing our list of high-quality books, call 1-800-542-2595 (USA) or 1-800-387-3178 (Canada).

Library of Congress Cataloging-in-Publication Data

Kiely Miller, Barbara.
Frederick Douglass / by Barbara Kiely Miller.
p. cm. — (Great Americans)
Includes bibliographical references and index.
ISBN-13: 978-0-8368-8315-2 (lib. bdg.)
ISBN-13: 978-0-8368-8322-0 (softcover)
ISBN-10: 0-8368-8315-2 (lib. bdg.)
ISBN-10: 0-8368-8322-5 (softcover)
1. Douglass, Frederick, 1818-1895—Juvenile literature. 2. African American abolitionists—Biography—Juvenile literature. 3. Abolitionists—United States—Biography—Juvenile literature. 4. Antislavery movements—United States—History—19th century—Juvenile literature. 5. Slaves—United States—Biography—Juvenile literature. I. Title.
E449.D75K54 2008
973.7'114092—dc22 2007008082

This edition first published in 2008 by
Weekly Reader® Books
An imprint of Gareth Stevens Publishing
1 Reader's Digest Road
Pleasantville, NY 10570-7000 USA

Managing editor: Valerie J. Weber
Art direction: Tammy West
Cover design and page layout: Charlie Dahl
Picture research: Sabrina Crewe
Production: Jessica Yanke

Picture credits: Cover, title page, pp. 6, 7, 8, 11, 14, 15, 20 (top) The Granger Collection, New York; p. 5 © North Wind Picture Archives; pp. 10, 20 (bottom) Courtesy National Park Service Museum Management Program and Frederick Douglass National Historical Site; pp. 12, 18 Charlie Dahl/© Gareth Stevens, Inc.; p. 16 Library of Congress; p. 19 Moorland-Spingarn Research Center; p. 21 © Lee Snider/Photo Images/Corbis.

Printed in the United States of America

1 2 3 4 5 6 7 8 9 11 10 09 08 07

Table of Contents

Cover and title page: Frederick Douglass was born into slavery and became a respected anti-slavery leader, speaker, and writer.

Chapter 1

A Young Leader

Frederick Douglass was nervous as he faced the crowd. It was August 16, 1841 and his first **anti-slavery** speech to white people. Douglass talked about his life as a **slave**. He described a slave's daily hunger and thin, ragged clothing. He told the crowd how his owner had beaten him. Nothing was worse, however, than being taken away from his family.

© North Wind Picture Archives

Douglass's descriptions of life as a slave convinced many white people that slavery must end.

The crowd stood and cheered. Douglass's words had painted a terrible picture of slavery. Slavery had to end now! Frederick Douglass's speeches and newspaper stories would make him into a powerful leader. He would spend his life helping African Americans, women, and other people become free and be treated fairly.

This picture from 1855 shows slaves working on a tobacco plantation, which were common in Maryland.

Frederick was born in February 1818 near Easton, Maryland. His mother was a slave named Harriet Bailey. Frederick Bailey never knew who his father, a white man, was. Harriet had to work in the fields of a **plantation** from morning until night. She sent baby Frederick to live with his grandparents nearby.

When Frederick turned six, he went to still another plantation. He had little food, no bed, and torn clothes. He saw other slaves beaten badly. Without his grandmother to watch over him, Frederick was afraid.

Then the man who owned Frederick sent him to work for a family in Baltimore, which was many miles away. Frederick was only eight years old, and he would live among total strangers.

Frederick's mother saw him one last time before he left for Baltimore. She became angry with the cook for not giving Frederick enough to eat.

Teaching slaves to read was against the law. In Baltimore, however, the woman that Frederick worked for taught him the alphabet. Soon he learned to spell and began reading newspapers and books. Frederick read about **abolitionists**, people who wanted to end slavery. He, too, wanted his freedom some day.

Mrs. Sophia Auld taught Frederick to read. When her husband found out, he stopped Frederick's lessons.

Chapter 2

Escape from Slavery

In 1833, Frederick was fifteen years old, tall, and strong. He was sent to work on another plantation. For three years, Frederick worked hard in the fields. He was beaten many times. After going to jail for trying to escape, Frederick was sent back to Baltimore.

Then Frederick began working in his owner's **shipyard**. He joined a **debate** club of **freed** blacks. There, he met a freed woman named Anne Murray. Frederick wanted to marry her, but he also wanted his freedom. He made a plan. Baltimore was close to Pennsylvania, where slavery was against the law. Could he get to Pennsylvania?

Anna Murray sold some of her belongings so Frederick could buy a train ticket.

If he wanted to escape, Frederick could not look like a slave. He borrowed a sailor's clothes. To travel, he would also need to prove he was free. A freed black sailor lent Frederick his papers stating he was a U.S. **citizen**. Frederick bought his train ticket for Pennsylvania. He hoped he would not be caught.

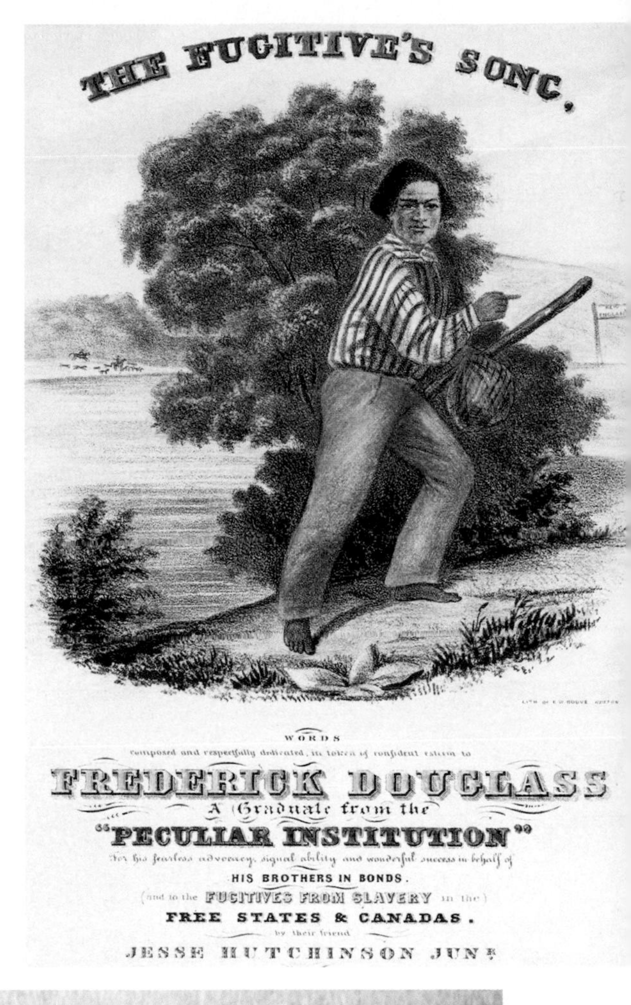

This drawing is from an 1845 song about abolition. The artist imagined what Douglass's escape from slavery was like.

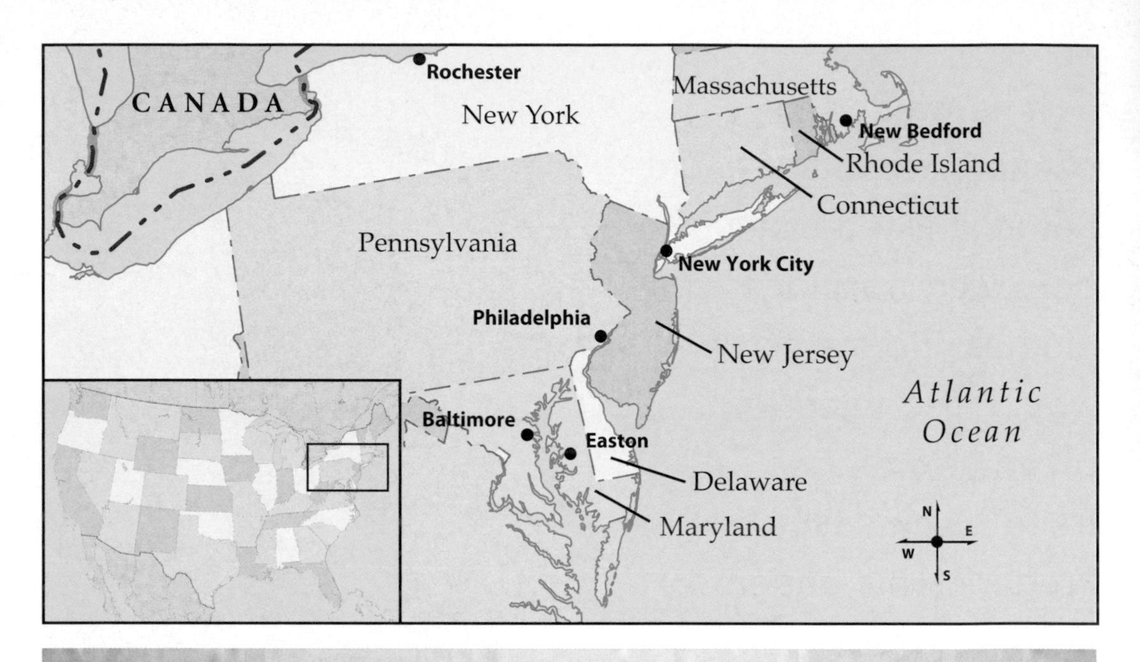

On September 3, 1838, Douglass escaped from slavery in Baltimore, Maryland, for freedom in northern cities.

The train **conductor** took Frederick's ticket. He looked at the borrowed papers but quickly moved on. Frederick was safe! He traveled on to New York City. When Anna arrived, they got married. They soon moved to New Bedford, Massachusetts. To hide from slave hunters, Frederick changed his last name from Bailey to Douglass.

Chapter 3

A Voice for Freedom

Soon after that first speech, the Massachusetts Anti-Slavery **Society** hired Frederick Douglass to give talks against slavery. Douglass became famous for his speeches throughout the northern states. He spoke out strongly for the right for everyone to be free and to be able to vote.

In 1845, Douglass published a book about his life, using his real name. Now he was in danger. Slave hunters might track him down and make him a slave again.

Newspaper ads like this one were used to try to catch slaves who had escaped.

$150 REWARD

RANAWAY from the subscriber, on the night of the 2d instant, a negro man, who calls himself *Henry May*, about 22 years old, 5 feet 6 or 8 inches high, ordinary color, rather chunky built, bushy head, and has it divided mostly on one side, and keeps it very nicely combed; has been raised in the house, and is a first rate dining-room servant, and was in a tavern in Louisville for 18 months. I expect he is now in Louisville trying to make his escape to a free state, (in all probability to Cincinnati, Ohio.) Perhaps he may try to get employment on a steamboat. He is a good cook, and is handy in any capacity as a house servant. Had on when he left, a dark cassinett coatee, and dark striped cassinett pantaloons, new—he had other clothing. I will give $50 reward if taken in Louisvill; 100 dollars if taken

After Douglass (*seated left of the woman in bonnet*) returned from Great Britain, he met with other abolitionists in New York.

To stay safe, Douglass sailed to Great Britain where he gave talks about slavery. He made many friends who raised money for him. In 1847, Douglass returned to the United States with the funds to buy his freedom. He paid $711.66 to his owner. At last, Frederick Douglass was a free man!

THE NORTH STAR.

ROCHESTER, N. Y., FRIDAY, JUNE 2, 1848.

Douglass and his family moved to Rochester, New York. There Douglass began his own newspaper and printed stories by black men and women.

Rochester was close to Canada where slavery was against the law. Douglass helped many slaves trying to escape to freedom in Canada.

Douglass's newspaper was named *The North Star*. It came out once a week.

Chapter 4

Advising the President

For years, Americans had argued over slavery. Many people in southern states did not want slavery to end. These states broke away from the United States. President Abraham Lincoln wanted to keep the country together, however. In 1861, the northern and southern states began the **Civil War**.

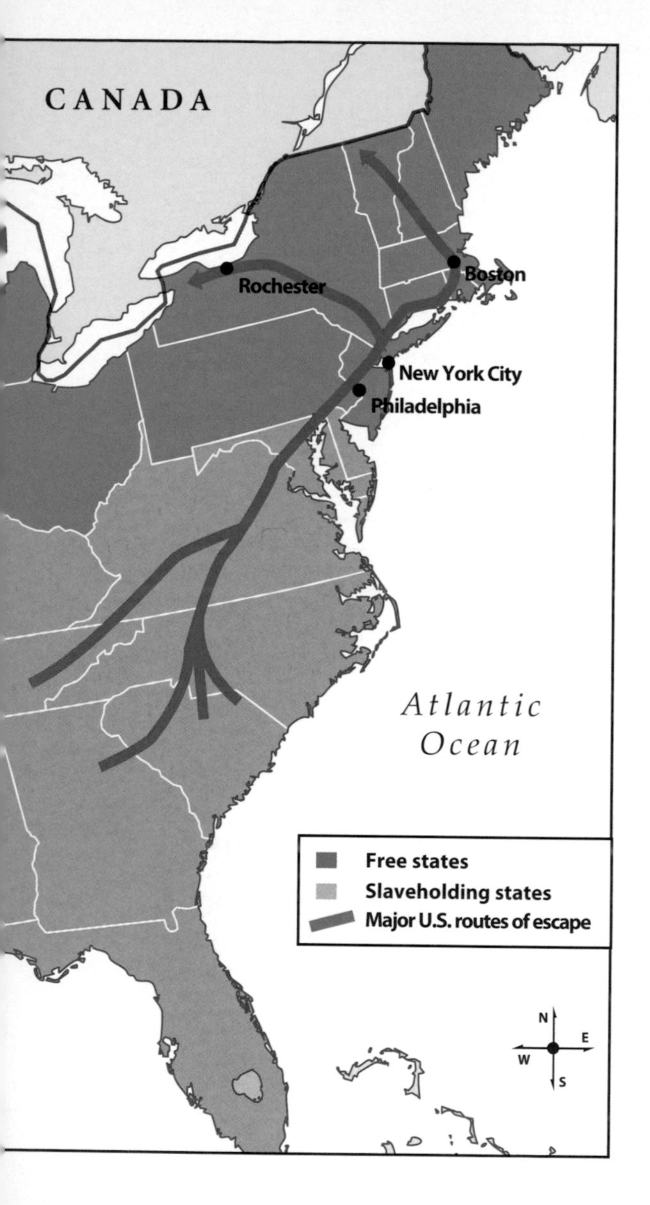

Douglass met with the president and helped convince Lincoln that the war should also end slavery. On December 31, 1862, President Lincoln announced to the country that the slaves in southern states were now free.

Many freed slaves came north to fight in the war. Douglass helped form a group of soldiers made up of all freed blacks.

This map shows some of the states that allowed slavery and some that did not.

The black soldiers were paid only half as much as white soldiers. The white soldiers also received more training and better weapons than the black soldiers did. Again, Douglass argued for equal treatment and asked Lincoln for help. In 1864, black soldiers were given equal pay and the supplies they needed.

Douglass's sons Lewis (*right*) and Charles were among the first to join a group of black soldiers from Massachusetts.

In 1865, the northern states won the war. On December 18, 1865, **Congress** ended slavery. In 1870, it said men of all races could vote.

After the war, Frederick Douglass and his family moved to Washington, D.C. He wrote another book about his life and held many government jobs.

Douglass wrote many speeches and articles from the library in his home.

Women still could not vote, however. Douglass knew many of the women fighting to change this. On February 20, 1895, he gave a speech supporting women. He was seventy-seven years old. Later that same day, he died. To his last breath, Frederick Douglass fought for the freedom and rights of all people.

Susan B. Anthony was a leader in the fight to gain women the right to vote. She and Douglass were friends. This sculpture shows them talking and drinking tea.

Glossary

abolitionists — people who did not believe people should be slaves and who worked to free slaves and end slavery

anti-slavery — against having people work without pay or freedom

citizen — an official member of a country who is given certain rights, such as voting and freedom of speech.

Civil War — the American war fought between Northern and Southern states from 1861 to 1865

conductor — the person who collects the tickets or payments from passengers on a train

Congress — the part of the U.S. government that makes laws

debate — a discussion of people's different ideas and why they are for or against something

freed — describes people who are no longer slaves and their children

plantation — a large area of land that is farmed

shipyard — a place where ships are built or repaired

slave — a person who is treated as property and is forced to work without pay. A slave does not have freedom.

society — a group of people who share the same interest

For More Information

Books

Frederick Douglass. Compass Point Early Biographies (series). Dana Meachen Rau (Capstone Press)

Frederick Douglass. First Biographies (series). Lola M. Schaefer (Capstone Press)

Frederick Douglass. Raintree Biographies (series). Patricia Lantier (Raintree)

Frederick Douglass: Voice for Freedom. Fact Finders (series). Kremena Spengler (Capstone Press)

Web Sites

America's Story: Frederick Douglass
www.americaslibrary.gov/cgi-bin/page.cgi/aa/douglass
Read about the important events in Frederick Douglass's life.

Pathways to Freedom: Maryland & the Underground Railroad
pathways.thinkport.org/following
Travel with two slave children who escape to freedom.

Publisher's note to educators and parents: Our editors have carefully reviewed these Web sites to ensure that they are suitable for children. Many Web sites change frequently, however, and we cannot guarantee that a site's future contents will continue to meet our high standards of quality and educational value. Be advised that children should be closely supervised whenever they access the Internet.

Index

About the Author

Barbara Kiely Miller is an editor and writer of educational books for children. She has a degree in creative writing from the University of Wisconsin–Milwaukee. Barbara lives in Shorewood, Wisconsin, with her husband and their two cats Ruby and Sophie. When she is not writing or reading books, Barbara enjoys photography, bicycling, and gardening.